21st Century Junior Library

MAKING AND KEEPING FRIENDS

Read and Reflect:
A Social-Emotional Guide

Emily Rose

Published in the United States of America by:

CHERRY LAKE PRESS
2395 South Huron Parkway, Suite 200, Ann Arbor, Michigan 48104
www.cherrylakepress.com

Reading Adviser: Beth Walker Gambro, MS, Ed., Reading Consultant, Yorkville, IL
Photo Credits: © Roman Samborskyi/Shutterstock.com, cover, 1, 20, 21; © wavebreakmedia/Shutterstock.com, 5, 17; © ViDI Studio/Shutterstock.com, 6; © TheVisualsYouNeed/Shutterstock.com, 7; © Hogan Imaging/Shutterstock.com, 8, 9; © Luis Molinero/Shutterstock.com, 10; © Beneda Miroslay/Shutterstock.com, 11 [right]; © Aries.P/Shutterstock.com, 11 [left]; © LightFieldStudios/Shutterstock.com, 12; © Odua Images/Shutterstock.com, 15; © Monkey Business Images/Shutterstock.com, 16; © This Is Me/Shutterstock.com, 18; © Meowlina Meow/Shutterstock.com, 19

Cherry Lake Press is an imprint of Cherry Lake Publishing Group.

Library of Congress Cataloging-in-Publication Data

Names: Rose, Emily (School psychologist), author.
Title: Making and keeping friends / by Emily Rose.
Description: Ann Arbor, Michigan : Cherry Lake Publishing, [2022] | Series: Read and reflect: a social-emotional guide | Includes bibliographical references and index. | Audience: Grades 2-3
Identifiers: LCCN 2021036559 (print) | LCCN 2021036560 (ebook) | ISBN 9781534199101 (hardcover) | ISBN 9781668900246 (paperback) | ISBN 9781668906002 (ebook) | ISBN 9781668901687 (pdf)
Subjects: LCSH: Friendship in children—Juvenile literature. | Friendship—Juvenile literature.
Classification: LCC BF723.F68 R65 2022 (print) | LCC BF723.F68 (ebook) | DDC 155.9/25—dc23
LC record available at https://lccn.loc.gov/2021036559
LC ebook record available at https://lccn.loc.gov/2021036560

Cherry Lake Press would like to acknowledge the work of the Partnership for 21st Century Learning, a Network of Battelle for Kids. Please visit http://www.battelleforkids.org/networks/p21 for more information.

Printed in the United States of America
Corporate Graphics

CHERRY LAKE PRESS

CONTENTS

Why Do We Need Friends? 4

How to Make Friends 8

How to Keep Friends 13

How to Know When You Have Outgrown a Friend 16

Extend Your Learning 20

Glossary 22

Find Out More 23

Index 24

About the Author 24

WHY DO WE NEED FRIENDS?

It is more fun to do things with other people than to do them alone. That's what friends are for! Having friends helps us learn about other people. Different people like different things, like games, foods, **hobbies**, TV shows, and even hairstyles. Having friends who like different things than we do can help us to try new things. That is **exciting**!

How do you practice being a good friend?

You might also have friends who like the same things that you like. Maybe you are friends with other kids on your soccer team or in your art class because each of you loves soccer or art. Having friends with similar **interests** means you can share something you love while spending time together.

What do you and your best friend have in common?

What is something you like to do with a friend?

Having friends can also be **comforting**. Your friend might sit next to you at lunch in the school cafeteria. They may ask to give you a hug when you feel sad. It's good to have friends and to be a friend!

Make a Guess!

In this chapter, we talked about some benefits of having friends, like trying new things and having someone there for you when you need it. What other benefits do friends bring?

HOW TO MAKE FRIENDS

One of the best ways to make friends is to try new things and **introduce** yourself to others. For example, your parents might sign you up for a summer science camp because you want to learn about science. There will probably be lots of kids at the camp who also like science. These kids could be great new friends!

You can start to make friends by telling the other kids your name and asking what their names are. Then you could

Practice introducing yourself to a new friend. What things would you say? An example could be something like, "Hi, my name is Tyshaun, and I like soccer. What games do you like?"

ask the other kids to do an activity together. Before you know it, you may have some new friends!

You might feel **nervous** before making new friends. This feeling is normal. Just remember that the other kids

Think!

Do you find it easy or hard to make new friends? If you find it hard, write down some things you can do that might make it easier.

probably feel nervous about making new friends too, so you already have something in common! Take a deep breath and remember that you can still introduce yourself and try new things *even when* you feel nervous. That is called having **confidence**, which is a good skill to practice.

What activities do you like to do? Think of some ways you can get involved in those activities and meet new friends who also like them.

How do you put effort into your friendships? Think about times you played a game that your friend wanted to play or when you talked about something your friend wanted to discuss.

HOW TO KEEP FRIENDS

True friendship can take some **effort**. Effort doesn't mean that friendship isn't fun. It means that you care enough about your friends to make them a **priority**. For example, you and your friend might play Chutes and Ladders every Tuesday after school. But one Tuesday, your friend might say that he wants to play Scrabble instead. Even if you don't like Scrabble as much, it's good to do what your friend is interested in sometimes too. After all, you would want your friend to say yes to trying a new game with you too, right?

This is an example of **compromise**, which is what good friendship is all about! A good friend always shares, takes turns, tries new things, and apologizes when they hurt their friend's feelings.

Ask Questions!

Have you ever had a friend that you don't really see anymore or talk to as much at school? Do you still like the same things, or have your interests changed?

What ways do you like to practice being a good friend? Think of your very best friend. What things do they do that make them a good friend to you?

HOW TO KNOW WHEN YOU HAVE OUTGROWN A FRIEND

Sometimes you might be friends with someone for a very long time. Other times you might notice that you and a friend don't really like the same things anymore.

What do you and your friends like to do together? Is that different from what you liked to do a few years ago?

People change over time. They learn new things and grow from new **experiences**.

Even though this is normal, it may mean that you and a friend might not have as much in common. Spending time together might not be as fun as it used to be. It can feel sad to outgrow a friend, but it helps to remember that you will also make new friends as you grow and change.

Look!

Look at a photo of you and an old friend. What do you remember about the day it was taken? How were you feeling?

We might have different friends at different stages of our lives. You probably had different friends in kindergarten than you will have in middle school. That's true for most people. But it is extra special when you have a friend or two that you love to spend time with as you grow up.

EXTEND YOUR LEARNING

Let's imagine your parents sign you up for a summer camp. You don't know anyone who will be there. Take a minute to think and write about how you feel.

Do you feel nervous, excited, or maybe a little bit of both?

If you feel nervous, think of another time when you were nervous about making new friends. What did you do then to feel better? What worked to make a friend, and what maybe didn't work so well?

Since you don't know anyone at the imaginary summer camp yet, what could you do to introduce yourself to other kids at the camp? Write about what activities you enjoy and how you might invite someone else to enjoy them with you.

Remember that every friend you have now, you once had to meet for the first time! It's okay if not everyone you meet becomes your friend. But trying new things and meeting new people is the best way to make new friends!

GLOSSARY

benefits (BEH-nuh-fits) things that are good for us

comforting (KUHM-fuhrt-ing) something that makes you feel better

compromise (KAHM-pruh-mize) settling differences and coming to a decision that works for everyone

confidence (KAHN-fuh-duhns) trust, belief in yourself

effort (EH-fuhrt) work or attention

exciting (ik-SYE-ting) something that is fun or great

experiences (ik-SPEER-ee-uhn-sez) things you have done or seen during your life

hobbies (HAH-beez) activities that you enjoy doing

interests (IN-tuh-rusts) things you like to do

introduce (in-truh-DOOSS) to present yourself to another person to get to know each other

nervous (NUHR-vuhss) uneasy or worried

priority (pry-OR-uh-tee) something that is important

FIND OUT MORE

Books

Bush, Zack, and Laurie Friedman. *The Little Book of Friendship.* Coral Gables, FL: Publishing Power, 2020.

Crohn, JoAnn. *Me and My Friendships.* Emeryville, CA: Rockridge Press, 2021.

Ferry, Beth. *Stick and Stone.* Boston, MA: Houghton Mifflin Harcourt, 2015.

Websites

Experience Friendship around the World!

https://oneglobekids.org
One Globe Kids connects you to other kids all around the world. Find a pen pal and learn about others with this fun organization.

YouTube—Friendship Soup Recipe: A NED Short

https://www.youtube.com/watch?v=H7w7yXkJTu0
Learn about the ingredients in friendship soup!

INDEX

apologizing, 14

changes, 17
comfort, 7
common interests, 6, 11, 17
compromise, 14
confidence, 11

effort, 12, 13
experiences, new, 17

friends
  changing, 16–19
  extending your learning, 20–21
  how to keep them, 12–15
  how to make them, 8–11
  importance of, 4–7
  outgrowing, 16–19

interests, similar, 6, 11, 17
introducing yourself, 8–11, 21

nervousness, 10–11, 20

priorities, 13

sharing, 14

taking turns, 14
trying new things, 8, 13–14, 21

ABOUT THE AUTHOR

Emily Rose is a school psychologist, yoga teacher, and writer for her mental wellness blog, MissMagnoliaSays.com. She enjoys helping kids and adults understand and manage their emotions and live beautiful lives. Emily lives in Dearborn, Michigan.